■ SCHOLASTIC

Building Essential Language Arts Skills

GRADE 4

D1225968

New York • Toronto • London • Auckland • Sydney
Mexico City • New Delhi • Hong Kong • Buenos Aires

Writer: Tina Posner
Editors: Maria L. Chang, Judy Kentor Schmauss
Cover design: Tannaz Fassihi; Cover art: Ana Bermejo
Interior design: Shekhar Kapur, Michelle H. Kim; Interior art: QBS Learning
Produced with QBS Learning

ISBN: 978-0-545-85036-0
Copyright © 2016 by Scholastic Inc.
All rights reserved. Printed in the U.S.A.
First printing, June 2016.

1 2 3 4 5 6 7 8 9 10   40   22 21 20 19 18 17 16

Table of Contents

Introduction

Help students master key language arts skills with this standards-based workbook, designed to help them become successful readers and writers. Fun and engaging reproducible activity pages provide targeted practice on important skills and concepts, such as parts of speech, capitalization, punctuation, spelling, domain-specific vocabulary, and so much more.

The ready-to-go practice pages in *Building Essential Language Arts Skills* are versatile and can be used in different ways:

- Select a skills page and use it as a "do now" activity to help students get settled first thing in the morning. Simply stack copies of the page on your desk for students to pick up as they enter the room and give the class five minutes to complete the activity.

- Preview the day's lesson with an appropriate skills page to find out what students already know about the topic.

- Alternatively, you can also use a skills page to review a recent lesson and assess what students have learned and what still needs further instruction.

- Assign pages for homework or independent work as needed.

An answer key is provided at the back of the book so you can review answers with the whole class. In doing so, you provide students with opportunities for discussion, reinforcement, or extension to other lessons. You may also want to encourage students to discuss their answers and strategies in small groups. This collaboration enables students to deepen their understanding or clarify any misunderstandings they may have about the skill or concept.

Meeting the Common Core State Standards

The activities in this workbook meet the following Common Core State Standards for English Language Arts. For more information about the standards, go to http://www.corestandards.org/ELA-Literacy.

Grade 4 Reading: Foundational Skills

RF.4.3 Know and apply grade-level phonics and word analysis skills in decoding words.

RF.4.3.a Use combined knowledge of all letter-sound correspondences, syllabication patterns, and morphology (e.g., roots and affixes) to read accurately unfamiliar multisyllabic words in context and out of context.

Grade 4 Language Skills

L.4.1 Demonstrate command of the conventions of standard English grammar and usage when writing or speaking.

L.4.1.a Use relative pronouns (*who, whose, whom, which, that*) and relative adverbs (*where, when, why*).

L.4.1.b Form and use the progressive verb tenses.

L.4.1.c Use modal auxiliaries (e.g., *can, may, must*) to convey various conditions.

L.4.1.d Order adjectives within sentences according to conventional patterns.

L.4.1.e Form and use prepositional phrases.

L.4.1.f Produce complete sentences, recognizing and correcting inappropriate fragments and run-ons.

L.4.1.g Correctly use frequently confused words.

L.4.2 Demonstrate command of the conventions of standard English capitalization, punctuation, and spelling when writing.

L.4.2.a Use correct capitalization.

L.4.2.b Use commas and quotation marks to mark direct speech and quotations from a text.

L.4.2.c Use a comma before a coordinating conjunction in a compound sentence.

L.4.2.d Spell grade-appropriate words correctly, consulting references as needed.

L.4.3 Use knowledge of language and its conventions when writing, speaking, reading, or listening.

L.4.3.a Choose words and phrases to convey ideas precisely.

L.4.3.c Differentiate between contexts that call for formal English and situations where informal discourse is appropriate.

L.4.4 Determine or clarify the meaning of unknown and multiple-meaning words and phrases based on grade 4 reading and content, choosing flexibly from a range of strategies.

L.4.4.a Use context as a clue to the meaning of a word or phrase.

L.4.4.b Use common, grade-appropriate Greek and Latin affixes and roots as clues to the meaning of a word.

L.4.4.c Consult reference materials, both print and digital, to find the pronunciation and determine or clarify the precise meaning of key words and phrases and to identify alternate word choices in all content areas.

L.4.5 Demonstrate understanding of figurative language, word relationships, and nuances in word meanings.

L.4.5.a Explain the meaning of simple similes and metaphors in context.

L.4.5.b Recognize and explain the meaning of common idioms, adages, and proverbs.

L.4.5.c Demonstrate understanding of words by relating them to their opposites (antonyms) and to words with similar but not identical meanings (synonyms).

L.4.6 Acquire and use accurately grade-appropriate general academic and domain-specific words and phrases, including those that signal precise actions, emotions, or states of being and that are basic to a particular topic.

Name: _____ Date: _____

A **pronoun** takes the place of a noun. For example: *Sara has a dog. She has a dog.*
A **relative pronoun** connects a clause or a phrase to a noun or pronoun. The words *who* and *that* are relative pronouns. Use *who* for people and *that* for animals, groups of people, and things.
For example: *Students who study get good grades. Animals that are small make good pets.*

The Tomato That Ate Cleveland

Connect the subject to the correct relative pronoun.
The first one has been done for you.

1. The tomato   that fell off the shelf

2. The baseball player   that ate Cleveland

3. The cat   who made stone soup

4. The books   who struck out at bat

5. The cooks   that wore a hat

Fill in the correct relative pronoun.

6. A song _____ won't stop playing in your head is called an earworm.

7. Friends _____ are loyal offer help when you need it.

8. The baseball team _____ plays at home will bat last.

Name: _____ Date: _____

 A **relative pronoun** connects a clause or a phrase to a noun or pronoun. The words *that* and *which* are relative pronouns. Use *that* for necessary information and *which* for extra information. Separate extra information from the sentence with commas. Test the information by saying the sentence without the relative pronoun. If the sentence still makes sense, then the information is not necessary.

Is That Really Necessary?

Choose the correct relative pronoun (*that* or *which*) for each sentence. Hint: Look to see if there is a comma before the blank.

On game days, we all dress in blue shirts. We like to wear the

color _____ represents our school. We all go to the
　　　　　　(1)

games, _____ are a pretty big deal in our town.
　　　　　　(2)

On the day we were playing our biggest rivals, a kid from our school showed up in yellow,

_____ is our rivals' color. People thought he wanted the other team to win
　　　　(3)

because he wore the color _____ represents them. But in the end, we won,
　　　　　　　　　　　　　　　　(4)

_____ made everyone forget about the color of our shirts!
　　　(5)

Correct this paragraph. Add commas where they belong.

Someone said we should all wear blue hats which was a silly idea. A blue shirt is
something that many people already have. But none of us have blue hats which we'd have
to buy with our allowances. Some of us don't even get allowances! And you can have school
spirit without looking like everyone else which is the point anyway.

The relative pronoun **whose** is a possessive form of *who*. It introduces a noun phrase. **Who's** is a contraction of *who is*.
For example: *Who's missing whose shoes?*

Who's Missing Whose Shoes?

Write *whose* or *who's* in each blank.
Hint: Try the words *who is* in each blank and see if they make sense.

1. Tommy, _____ shoes are under the bed, is not ready for school.

2. Tommy, _____ looking for his shoes, is going to be late.

3. Tommy, _____ feet are probably cold, really needs his shoes.

4. Tommy's mother, _____ getting impatient, is telling him to hurry.

5. Tommy, _____ teacher is strict about lateness, has been warned before.

6. Tommy, _____ always losing his shoes, had promised to be more careful!

Progressive tense verbs are verbs that show ongoing or repeated actions. The actions can happen now, in the past, or in the future. To make the progressive tense, add *-ing* to a verb. You might have to drop the final *-e* or double the final consonant before adding *-ing*.
For example: *I am <u>hoping</u> my bunny will soon get tired of <u>hopping</u> all over my bed.*

I Am Fishing!

Fill in the blanks by adding *-ing* to the given verb.

1. The girl is _____ *(try)* to catch a fish.

2. She keeps _____ *(throw)* her line into the water.

3. She is _____ *(wait)* patiently, but nothing is _____ *(bite)*.

4. Hold on! She is _____ *(feel)* something!

5. She is _____ *(tug)* and _____ *(pull)* on the line.

6. She was _____ *(hope)* that she got a fish.

7. Yes! She will be _____ *(have)* fish for dinner!

Building Essential Language Arts Skills: Grade 4 © Scholastic Inc.

The **conditional tense** is used for things that didn't or might not happen. Remember to use the helping verb *to have* with a past participle after the words *could, should, would,* and *might.* For example: I *could have used* more sunscreen!

I Should Have Used the Conditional

Underline the verb in the first sentence. Then use that verb to make the second sentence conditional. The first one has been done for you.

1. I <u>was</u> not careful at the beach yesterday.

I should ___**have been**___ more careful at the beach yesterday.

2. I fell asleep on the blanket.

I shouldn't _____ asleep on the blanket.

3. Someone threw a towel over me.

Someone could _____ a towel over me.

4. I didn't leave the beach early.

I would _____ the beach early.

5. I played under the umbrella.

I might _____ under the umbrella.

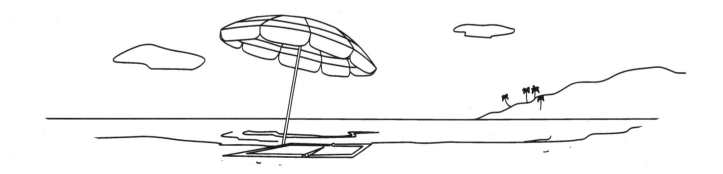

> There is an order to follow when using more than one adjective to describe a noun. Look at the chart below for the correct order to put them in. When you use adjectives in the correct order, you can leave out a comma between them.
> For example: *John has a big brown dog.*

Ordering Up Insults

Fill in the chart with more adjectives that fit each category.

Quantity	Opinion	Age/Size/Shape/Color	Origin	Material
a/an	smelly	old	Martian	leathery

Now use the adjectives in your chart to order up some funny foods.

1. That was _____ _____ _____ chicken
   (quantity)   *(age/size/shape/color)*   *(material)*
   we had for dinner.

2. We had _____ _____ _____ milk to drink.
   (quantity)   *(opinion)*   *(opinion)*

3. Then for dessert we tried _____ _____
   (quantity)   *(age/size/shape/color)*
   _____ pie(s).
   (opinion)

4. It was the worst _____ _____ _____
   (opinion)   *(origin)*   *(material)*
   meal I ever had!

Building Essential Language Arts Skills: Grade 4 © Scholastic Inc.

Name: _____   Date: _____

Prepositions are words that show location, such as <u>under</u> the desk or <u>next to</u> the chair.

Let's Go on a Field Trip

Follow the directions to go on a field trip. Trace your path on the map.
Circle all the prepositions that helped you get there.

Head down the street away from the school.

Go around the lake.

Go over the bridge.

Turn left at the traffic light.

Go under the bridge.

Follow the road into the traffic circle.

Exit on the opposite side of the circle.

Take the road through the park.

Where did you end up?

_____

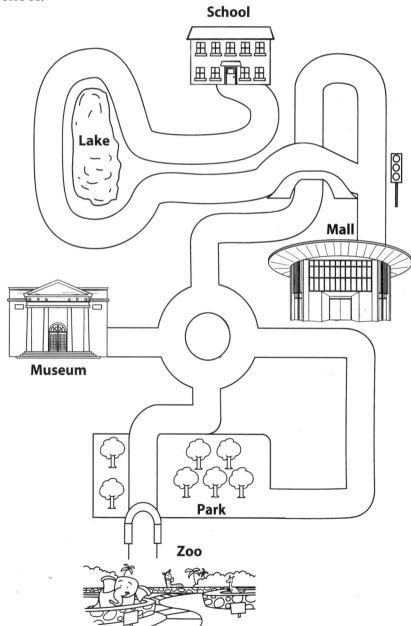

Building Essential Language Arts Skills: Grade 4 © Scholastic Inc.

Name: _____ Date: _____

 Prepositions can be used in expressions of time, such as _in_ the morning or _before_ Monday.

In the Morning on Monday

Circle the preposition that relates to time in each sentence.
Then find that preposition in the word search below.
Hint: Words can go across or down.

1. I woke up before 7:00 today.

2. I read during breakfast.

3. I brushed my teeth after I ate.

4. I left for school by 8:00.

5. I arrived in school ten minutes past 8:00.

6. Since we moved, I can walk to school.

7. I learn a lot throughout the day.

8. When I get home, I do my homework until dinnertime.

N	G	T	O	A	F	T	E	R	E
T	H	R	O	U	G	H	O	U	T
P	Y	B	E	F	O	R	E	M	H
A	T	H	R	G	L	N	C	B	X
S	V	X	Q	D	U	R	I	N	G
T	D	Y	S	I	N	C	E	A	E
S	Z	D	T	B	Y	S	F	S	O
G	G	M	U	N	T	I	L	W	Z

Building Essential Language Arts Skills: Grade 4 © Scholastic Inc.

A complete sentence has a subject and a verb, and it expresses a complete thought. A **sentence fragment** is incomplete.

Fix the Fragments

These fragments have created a disaster zone!
Match the fragments to create complete sentences.

1. A broken pipe flooded   the windstorm.

2. Rats chewing through a wire   through the wall.

3. Water on the floor   made it slippery.

4. A tree fell during   the basement.

5. A car came crashing   started a fire.

A **run-on sentence** is really two or more sentences without a break. Fix run-on sentences by adding a period or by combining them with a comma and a conjunction.

The Relay Race

Put a slash between each possible sentence.

The relay race is about to begin there are two teams racing the runners are all fast everyone is expecting an exciting race we'll cheer for them all we hope our school will win

Fix the run-on sentences with the conjunctions shown below.

1. _____ ,

   and _____ .

2. _____ ,

   so _____ .

3. _____ ,

   but _____ .

Building Essential Language Arts Skills: Grade 4 © Scholastic Inc.

Name: _____ Date: _____

 Some words look or sound alike but mean different things. For example: *to, too,* and *two.*

Copy Cats

Use the words in the box to fill in the blanks. You can use each word more than once.

> they're   there   their   two   to   too

Jamie and Maria said _____ going _____ a party.
(1)   (2)

They've decided _____ wear _____ blue sweaters.
(3)   (4)

All _____ friends are going _____. The party starts
(5)   (6)

at _____ P.M. They have to walk _____ the party
(7)   (8)

because _____ parents are busy. But the party is not
(9)

_____ far away, so they'll get _____ just in time.
(10)   (11)

Will you be _____ ?
(12)

Circle the correct word.

13. (*Your/You're*) shoes are so cute!

14. That's a great sweater (*your/you're*) wearing!

15. (*It's/Its*) color is perfect on you.

16. (*It's/Its*) new, right?

> ⭐ Some words sound alike but have different spellings and meanings. Many people get confused and use them incorrectly. Know what these words mean so you can use them correctly.
> For example: *Mom gave him quite a large piece of pie so we can finally have some peace and quiet.*

It's Quite Quiet in Here

Write a sentence for each word pair. Make sure to use the words correctly. The first one has been done for you.

1. accept/except

  I'll accept what you're saying, except I think you're wrong.

2. capital/capitol

_____

3. affect/effect

_____

4. its/it's

_____

5. then/than

_____

6. all ready/already

_____

Write the two words that solve this riddle.

What flies through the air and is like a pizza without toppings?

_____

Name: _____ Date: _____

Capital letters are needed at the beginning of each sentence and for proper names of people, places, and events.
For example: *Mary Draper of Massachusetts was a hero of the American Revolution.*

Capital Center

Underline the letters that should be capitalized in each sentence. The number next to the sentence tells you how many capital letters there should be.

1. would you like to visit the united states capitol? (4)

2. it is a familiar sight in washington, d.c. (4)

3. the building was designed by dr. william thornton in 1874. (4)

4. the capitol is where the u.s.
congress meets. (5)

5. the two bodies of congress are the senate
and the house of representatives. (5)

6. the first woman elected to congress was
jeannette rankin from montana. (5)

7. several african americans who were born into slavery were elected to congress
after the civil war. (6)

8. the youngest person ever elected to congress, elise stefanik of new york,
was 30 years old. (6)

⭐ Capitalize days of the week, months, and holidays.
For example: *Valentine's Day falls on a Sunday this February.*

Hilarious Holidays

Rewrite the sentences so words are capitalized correctly.

1. ahoy! talk like a pirate day is on september 19.

_____

2. dress like someone else on april 20 for look-alike day.

_____

3. may 2 is brothers and sisters day, so be nice!

_____

4. another date to circle is may 14 for dance like a chicken day!

_____

5. i can't wait to celebrate national ice cream day on july 21.

_____

6. on august 16, make someone laugh on national tell a joke day.

_____

7. january begins with new year's day and ends with backwards day!

_____

8. do your part to support national stop bullying day on october 6.

_____

Name: _____   Date: _____

 Use quotation marks to show the exact words that someone said.

Quotable Quotes

Use the clues to write the quote said by each famous person. Be sure to use quotation marks.

You miss 100% of the shots you don't take.

Freedom is never given; it is won.

The truth is always the strongest argument.

Adventure is worthwhile in itself.

Anyone who has never made a mistake has never tried anything new.

1. The scientist Albert Einstein, who was famous for his new ideas, once said,

_____

2. The pilot Amelia Earhart, who was famous for exploring, once said,

_____

3. Wayne Gretzky, a famous hockey player, once said,

_____

4. Sophocles, a famous thinker from Ancient Greece, once claimed,

_____

5. A. Philip Randolph, who fought for civil rights, once stated,

_____

> ⭐ Commas separate a quotation from the rest of the sentence.
> Use two commas unless some other punctuation ends the quote.
> For example: *President Franklin D. Roosevelt once said, "The only thing we have to fear is fear itself," and I agree.*

Comma Commando

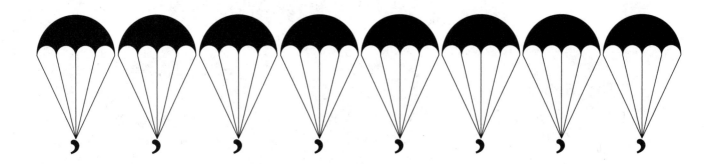

These eight commas are looking for a place to land. Put them into the sentences where they belong. The first one has been done for you.

1. Ava yelled ⌄ "Hey, Lamar. Guess what?"

2. Lamar answered "I can't guess."

3. "I invented a new game" said Ava.

4. "What's it called?" asked Lamar.

5. "It's called Comma Commando" Ava answered proudly.

6. "Comma Come Man who?" Lamar joked.

7. "Seriously" said Ava "do you want to play?"

8. "Well" Lamar said "it does look like fun."

Two sentences can be joined to form a compound sentence using a comma and a conjunction. For example: *That shirt is torn,* <u>*but*</u> *I can fix it.*

Stitching Sentences Together

Stitch these sentences together by choosing a conjunction from the box. Use each one twice.

> and   but   so

1. Finger knitting is easy to learn, _____ it is fun to do.

2. Finger knitting creates thin ropes, _____ you can stitch them together.

3. You might make mistakes at first, _____ you can learn how to fix them.

4. You can watch videos online, _____ it helps to see how to do new projects.

5. Yarn can be thick or thin, _____ choose the best one for your project.

6. Yarn can be expensive, _____ you can wait for a sale.

Now finish this sentence.

Finger knitting might be fun, _____.

Connect some short sentences together with a comma and a conjunction. A mix of short and longer sentences sounds best. Sentences that are all the same length sound boring and machine-like.

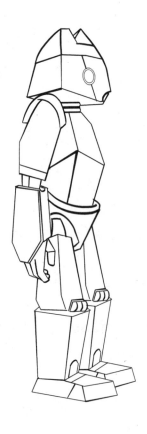

Don't Be a Robot

Read the paragraphs.

Paragraph 1:

Short sentences are bold. They can get your attention. Using all short sentences is boring. It sounds like a robot is talking. Try it. Read these sentences. Use a robot voice.

Paragraph 2:

An android is also a robot. It is designed to look and act like a human. A human would use some conjunctions. An android would use conjunctions, too. Short sentences are for robots.

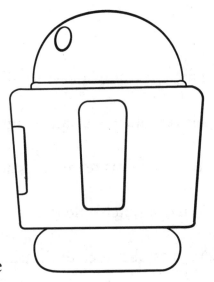

Now rewrite the second paragraph, using conjunctions to connect some of the sentences.

_____

_____

_____

_____

_____

_____

_____

Name: _____ Date: _____

 Modal verbs are used with other verbs to show possibility, ability, obligation, or permission. *Can* and *may* are modals. *Can* is most often used to show ability; *may* is most often used for permission. For example: *Can I lift this box? May I go to the movies?*

Can I Help You?

Circle the correct modal verb in each sentence.

1. *(Can/May)* I help you with your groceries?

2. I don't know if I *(can/may)* carry this heavy box.

3. I *(can/may)* play tennis, but I'm not very good.

4. Yes, she *(can/may)* go on vacation with us.

5. Zack took lessons and *(can/may)* sing beautifully.

6. *(Can/May)* I go to the movies tonight?

7. Henry *(can/may)* lift 50 pounds!

8. I will ask Mom if I *(can/may)* stay home today.

Name: _____ Date: _____

 Could, would, and **should** are also **modal verbs**. Use *could* for ability. Use *would* to talk about unlikely or unreal situations, or to make polite offers. Use *should* to talk about advice.

I Would if I Could

Write the missing word in each sentence. Choose from *would, could,* or *should*.

1. _____ you like me to help you move the piano?

2. You _____ talk it over with her before you make a decision.

3. Sam _____ learn Spanish before she travels to South America.

4. My dad _____ be happy to help you fix your car.

5. I _____ come over after school and help you study.

6. I wish I _____ sleep till noon!

7. You _____ read Robert Smith's new book!

8. If I were older, I _____ learn to drive.

Name: _____   Date: _____

 Some vowel sounds are not stressed and have the neutral sound /uh/.
This vowel sound is called **schwa**.
Examples: *mountain* (MOUN-tuhn), *again* (uh-GEN), *blossom* (BLOS-uhm)

Up the Mountain Again

Read aloud these pronunciations that have the schwa sound.
Spell the words. The first one has been done for you.

1. uh-SEND   ___ascend___

2. PLEZ-uhnt   _____

3. REE-uh-lize   _____

4. DIS-tuhnt   _____

5. FOS-uhl   _____

6. GRAV-uhl   _____

7. LOH-kuhl   _____

8. FLOR-uhl   _____

9. JEN-ur-uhs   _____

10. pruh-TEKT   _____

11. suh-PORT   _____

12. TIK-uhl   _____

Some words end in *-sion* and some words end in *-tion*.
Words that end in *-sion* usually have the /zhuhn/ sound, as in *television* or *occasion*.
Most words that end in *-tion* have the /shuhn/ sound, as in *operation* and *fraction*.

Operation Television

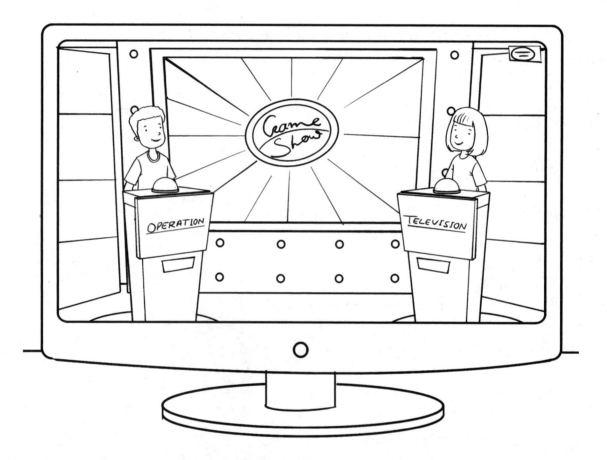

Add either *-sion* or *-tion* to complete each word.

1. vi_____

2. explo_____

3. subtrac_____

4. por_____

5. ten_____

6. loca_____

7. carna_____

8. deci_____

9. affec_____

10. confu_____

11. mis_____

12. condi_____

Name: _____   Date: _____

A Dear Deer

**Look at the pictures and clues and create a homophone for each.
The first one has been done for you.**

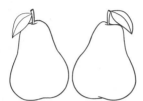

1. two fruits   <u>pair of pears</u>

2. an insect's   _____
mom's sister

3. a large mammal _____
without fur

4. a light-colored _____
bucket

Write a homograph that solves the clues.

5. This can be the sound a clock makes or a small annoying bug.   _____

6. This can be a short quick sound or another name for "Dad."   _____

7. This can be a line or what you do to move a canoe.   _____

8. This can be a sea mammal or what you do to an envelope.   _____

9. This can be the inside of your hand or a kind of tree.   _____

The letter *c* makes the /k/ sound, as in *cat*, and the /s/ sound, as in *celery*. But it can also make a /sh/ sound, as in *special*. In most of these words, an *i* follows the *c*. The letter *s* makes the /s/ sound, but it can also make the /z/ sound, as in *scissors*. These words have to be memorized.

My Special Scissors

Read the clues. Then unscramble the letters in parentheses to make words with a /z/ sound spelled with *s*. Write them on the line.

1. A gift (*nesprte*)   _____

2. Dairy food you put in a sandwich (*ecehes*)   _____

3. Tells or speaks (*ysas*)   _____

4. A tune or melody (*simuc*)   _____

5. A breaking story you hear or read about (*ewns*) _____

6. Something that can harm you if swallowed (*ioopsn*) _____

Use the words in the box to fill in the blanks.

> physician   glaciers   delicious   social   artificial   official

7. If something is manmade, it is _____.

8. You can find _____ in Antarctica and Greenland.

9. The rose is the _____ state flower of New York.

10. I want to be a _____ when I grow up.

11. My favorite subject in school is _____ studies.

12. Dad makes the most _____ muffins for breakfast.

Some words have silent letters, such as the *b* in *comb*, the *t* in *castle*, the *w* in *write*, and the *k* and *gh* in *knight*.

Silent Knight

shhhh ∫∫∫

Choose a letter from the box to complete the words.
Some letters are used more than once.

n	b	k	t	g	w	l

It was a cold Wed___esday in autum___. The ___night approached the cas___le
     (1)   (2)   (3)   (4)

and used a ha___f-___not to tie his horse to the gate. He went up to the door and
        (5)   (6)

put his thum___ on the doorbell, then lis___ened for footsteps. He had not noticed a
       (7)   (8)

si___n on the door. It said, "Do not ring the ___rong bell." Not ___nowing if he had
(9)   (10)   (11)

rung the ___rong bell or not, the ___night si___hed and wa___ked away.
     (12)   (13)   (14)   (15)

Name: _____   Date: _____

 Some words don't follow any spelling rules. You just have to memorize their spellings.

Spelling Is a Talent

Circle the misspelled words in the paragraph. Then spell them correctly on the lines below.

Jennifer and her frend Katy were practicing for the talent show. They were bizy and needed help getting reddy. "I have an idee," Jennifer sed. "My sister can help us. She goes to beuty skool." Katy replied, "Yay! Does that mean we have time to get peetza?"

_____   _____

_____   _____

_____   _____

_____   _____

Choose words that say precisely what you mean in an interesting way.
For example, you could say, "The bee flew around the flower."
But it would be more precise to say, "The bee *hovered* around the flower."
The word *hovered* tells how the bee flew and makes the sentence more interesting to read.

Bee Precise

Draw a line from each underlined word to a word that is more precise.

1. He is <u>nice</u>.   sobbing

2. It was a <u>cold</u> morning.   deafening

3. She is <u>funny.</u>   thoughtful

4. The meal was <u>good</u>.   grateful

5. The child was <u>crying</u>.   dazzling

6. I am <u>glad</u> to be on vacation.   frosty

7. The sunshine was <u>bright</u>.   witty

8. The machine was <u>loud</u>.   flavorful

Use one or two commas to set off a name, an exclamation, or a question in a sentence. For example: *Peter, wait for me. We're going to meet at the park, right?*

Tag Me In

Choose words from the box to fill in the blanks. Don't forget to use commas where needed.

> right   Samir   buddy   Wait   Wow   okay

1. _____ I've got an extra ticket to the wrestling match. Want to go?

2. _____ it's supposed to be an epic battle!

3. You should check with your parents first _____?

4. _____ how much do I owe you for the ticket?

5. You don't owe me anything _____ because my dad got them for free!

6. We're going to have such a great time _____?

Name: _____   Date: _____

 Slang expressions are fine when you're talking with your friends or close family. With teachers and other adults, avoid slang and use proper grammar.

In Good Form

Draw a line to match the speech bubbles with the speakers. Match the formal language with Joseph and the informal language with Joey. Then write how each boy might say goodbye in the empty bubbles.

Hello, how are you?

Got the time?

Hey, what's up?

I am not sure what time it is.

I am supposed to be home at five, too.

I've gotta be home by five, or else!

_____
_____
_____

_____
_____
_____

Joseph

Joey

Name: _____ Date: _____

⭐ When you come across an unfamiliar word, look for clues in the words that surround it.

Critter Crossword

Use the clues to fill in the boxes in this crossword puzzle.

band
buck
cackle
cob
flock
hatchling
joey
kid
pen
pod

Across

2. A baby turtle or alligator is called a _____, perhaps because it comes out of an egg.

5. It's a male swan, not corn.

7. You wouldn't guess that a group of camels is called a _____, the same as a group of birds.

8. You don't write with it, but it's what a female swan is called.

9. A young goat is called a _____, like a child.

Down

1. They may not be musical, but a group of gorillas is called a _____.

3. A group of hyenas is called a _____, maybe because of the laughing sound they make.

4. A baby koala is called a _____, like a baby kangaroo.

6. It's a male deer, not a dollar.

8. Dolphins swim in a _____, kind of like peas.

Name: _____ Date: _____

Context clues can help you choose between two words that sound the same.
For example, the words *eye* and *I* sound the same, but you wouldn't say: *Eye have something in my I.*

An I for an Eye!

Choose the best word from the box.

board	dear	flour	groan
bored	deer	flower	grown

1. The baker was covered in _____.

2. The hunter was waiting for a _____.

3. I fell asleep at the movie because I was _____.

4. Your baby brother is all _____ up now.

5. Let's put the pretty _____ in some water.

6. That woman isn't really my aunt; she's my mother's _____ friend.

7. The teacher wants us to write the answer on the _____.

8. The joke was bad, and you could hear the audience _____.

Name: _____ Date: _____

Going First!

Look at each underlined prefix and picture clue.
Write the meaning of the prefix on the line.

1. <u>sub</u>marine _____

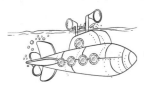

3. <u>fore</u>cast _____

2. <u>semi</u>circle _____

4. <u>super</u>size _____

Fill in the blanks. Use a prefix from the box.

> super-   sub-   semi-   fore-

5. In some cities, you can ride underground on the _____way.

6. Our basketball team didn't make it to the finals, but we did make it

to the _____finals.

7. Having _____sight means thinking ahead.

8. There are so many things you can buy at a _____market.

Notice how prefixes can change the meaning of a word.
For example: If the meat is *overdone*, it is past done. If the meat is *underdone*, it is not done enough.

Over and Under

Make six new words by adding the prefixes in the chart to each word in the box.

> feed   achieve   rated

over	under

Answer the questions by circling "Yes" or "No."

1. If you underfeed your pet fish, is it hungry?   Yes   No

2. If you overachieve on a spelling test, did you get a good grade?   Yes   No

3. If a movie is overrated, is it better than people say it is?   Yes   No

4. If you overfeed a dog regularly, will it lose weight?   Yes   No

5. If the home team underachieves, did they play a good game?   Yes   No

6. If a dessert is underrated, are you surprised that it's so good?   Yes   No

A **suffix**, which is a word part at the end of a word, can help you figure out the word's meaning.
The suffix *-er* means "person who," as in *worker*.
The suffix *-less* means "without," as in *helpless*.

At the End

Fill in the blanks with the suffix *-er* or *-less*.

1. We had a speak_____ on graduation day.

2. Ms. Jacobs is a great teach_____.

3. Our team was losing by a lot, so we were feeling hope_____.

4. After running really fast, you might be breath_____.

5. One of my friends is a sing_____ in the school chorus.

6. A wasp landed on her arm, but Debra was fear_____.

7. Have you read the story about the head_____ horseman?

8. You don't have to be tall to be a good basketball play_____.

Name: _____ Date: _____

A Meaningful Ending

Choose a suffix from the box to fill in the blanks.

-able = can be done (bendable)

-ful = a lot of something (playful)

-y = has this quality (bouncy)

1. We decided on our group project quickly because everyone was agree_____.

2. Danny set the table and did the dishes because he likes to be help_____.

3. Be care_____! Your shoes are untied!

4. The forecast says it will be cloud_____ today.

5. People said our team was very beat_____, but we haven't lost yet!

6. The vase of flowers looks very cheer_____ on the table.

7. The dog needs a bath because he is very dirt_____.

8. This candidate is popular, so the newspaper says she is elect_____.

9. That is a power_____ wind bending the trees!

10. Some people have curl_____ hair, and others have straight hair.

Name: _____   Date: _____

 A **word root** is a basic word to which prefixes and suffixes are added to make new words. Recognizing a word root inside a word can help you figure out its meaning.

Digging Up Roots

ROOTS

bio   geo   photo

1. Circle the words that contain the root that means "life."
Then use one of the circled words in a sentence.

biography   bingo   biology   business   biodegradable

_____

_____

2. Circle the words that contain the root that means "earth."
Then use one of the circled words in a sentence.

geology   gorgeous   geometry   geography   gigantic

_____

_____

3. Circle the words that contain the root that means "light."
Then use one of the circled words in a sentence.

phony   physical   photocopy   photograph   photosynthesis

_____

_____

Name: _____ Date: _____

Digging Up Roots (continued)

> **ROOTS**
>
> cent   aud   struct   tract

4. Circle the words that contain the root that means "100."
Then write another word that has this root.

certain   percent   purchase   century

_____

5. Circle the words that contain the root that means "hearing."
Then write another word that has this root.

audience   apply   August   audition

_____

6. Circle the words that contain the root that means "build."
Then write another word that has this root.

concert   construction   destruct   dessert

_____

7. Circle the words that contain the root that means "pulling or dragging."
Then write another word that has this root.

attention   attract   trace   tractor

_____

Name: _____ Date: _____

 A **syllable** is a word part that contains a vowel. Syllables can be open or closed.
In a **closed syllable**, the vowel is followed by a consonant and usually has a short sound.
For example: *cap•tain, fun•nel, med•al*
In an **open syllable**, the syllable ends with the vowel sound, which is usually long.
For example: *so•nar, o•pen, ba•by*

Syllable Sonar

Put a slash (/) between the syllables. Then circle "open" or "closed" to tell
what kind the first syllable is.

1. vapor	open	closed	
2. happen	open	closed	
3. engine	open	closed	
4. meter	open	closed	
5. spider	open	closed	
6. insect	open	closed	
7. problem	open	closed	
8. music	open	closed	
9. ugly	open	closed	
10. human	open	closed	
11. radar	open	closed	
12. object	open	closed	

Recognizing syllables helps you sound out unfamiliar words.
Remember, each syllable contains one vowel sound.
For example: *un•scram•bled* has three syllables.

Syllable Unscramble

Unscramble these syllables to form words. The first one has been done for you.

1.
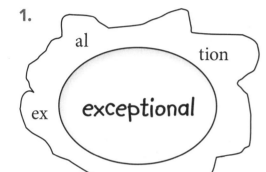
al
tion
ex
exceptional
cep

4.
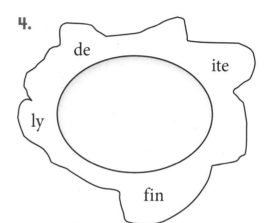
de
ite
ly
fin

2.
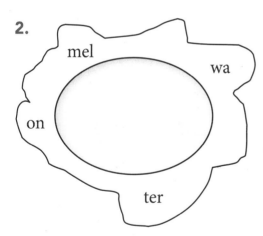
mel
wa
on
ter

5.
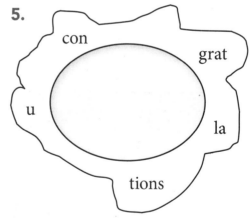
con
grat
u
la
tions

3.
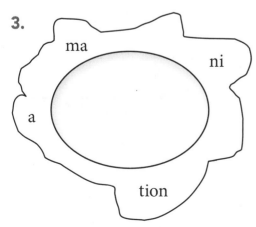
ma
ni
a
tion

6.
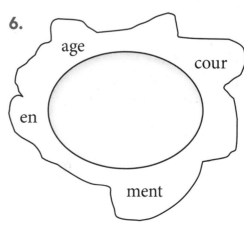
age
cour
en
ment

When you come across an unknown word, see if you can break it into parts.

Franken-Words

Sort the word parts into prefixes, roots, and suffixes.

cover	dis	ness
re	able	un
ed	mark	kind

1. prefixes

_____

_____

_____

2. roots

_____

_____

_____

3. suffixes

_____

_____

_____

Use the word parts to make three words.

_____   _____   _____

Name: _____ Date: _____

 The guide words at the top of a dictionary page tell the first and last words on that page. They help you find words in the dictionary.

Tour Guide

Circle all the words that you would find between each pair of guide words.

1. | choose | clean |

cancel   color   cry   city

4. | sharp | sick |

soda   satisfied   shadow   show

2. | embarrass | enough |

effort   empty   enter   end

5. | leave | leisure |

left   light   legend   lemon

3. | obey | ocean |

open   object   obvious   otter

6. | romantic | rough |

route   rosy   rotate   round

Name: _____ Date: _____

 A **simile** compares two different things that share one quality. It makes the comparison clear by using the words *like* or *as*.

Like Two Peas in a Pod

Look at the two underlined words. What do they have in common?
Complete the simile by adding a word that compares the two.
The first one has been done for you.

1. Her <u>smile</u> was as _____ bright _____ as <u>sunshine</u>.

2. The <u>leaves</u> _____ like <u>ballerinas</u>.

3. The <u>grass</u> felt as _____ as <u>velvet</u> on my bare feet.

4. The <u>cat</u> _____ like a <u>baby</u>.

5. The old <u>sneakers</u> were as _____ as a <u>garbage dump</u>.

6. His <u>fingers</u> were as _____ as <u>Popsicles</u>.

Name: _____ Date: _____

A **metaphor** compares two things, but does NOT use the words *like* or *as*.
It substitutes one thing for another in order to stress a similar quality.
For example: *The batter was a machine!* Here the quality stressed is "without human error."

Magnificent Metaphors

Answer the questions to analyze each metaphor.

1. Charlie was an **octopus** on the basketball court.

What is special about an octopus? _____

How would having this quality help a basketball player?_____

_____

2. Lara was a **cheetah** on the racetrack.

What quality about a cheetah is important here? _____

How would having this quality help a runner? _____

_____

More Metaphors

Write a sentence with a metaphor using each pair of words.
Remember NOT to use *like* or *as* in your comparisons.
The first one has been done for you.

1. 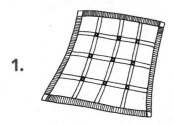   fog / blanket

The fog was a blanket over the land.

2.    air conditioning / freezer

_____

3.    car / dinosaur

_____

4.    child / fish

_____

Idioms are phrases that come from old sayings or stories. You can't tell what they mean by looking up the definition of each word in the phrase. For example: *Under the weather* means "not feeling well." It has nothing to do with rain or sunshine.

Do They Mean What They Say?

Next to each saying, write the letter that shows what the idiom means. You can use a reference book or the Internet to look up idioms you don't know.

1. Don't pull the wool over my eyes! _____

2. Don't judge a book by its cover. _____

3. We've missed the boat! _____

4. We let the cat out of the bag! _____

5. You hit the nail on the head! _____

6. You burned the midnight oil. _____

7. Time to hit the sack. _____

8. Time to jump on that bandwagon. _____

a. You got that exactly right.

b. Don't focus on the way something looks.

c. Don't try to fool me.

d. Time to go to bed.

e. We told a secret we shouldn't have.

f. You stayed up late working.

g. Time to join what others are doing.

h. We lost our chance.

Get My Meaning?

Circle the letter for the idiom that goes with each situation.
You can use a reference book or the Internet to look up idioms you don't know.

1. It's been a terrible day. You missed the bus to school. You had a surprise quiz.
   You come home from school, and your little brother ate all of the chips. You say,

   a. That's a hot potato!

   b. That's an arm and a leg!

   c. That's the last straw!

   d. That's a piece of cake!

2. You've joined the school soccer team. You are running for class president.
   And you're also the lead in the school play. Someone says,

   a. You've probably bitten off more than you can chew.

   b. Stop beating around the bush.

   c. Every cloud has a silver lining.

   d. You're barking up the wrong tree.

3. You played a practical joke on your best friend with an exploding pen.
   She got you back with some foaming chewing gum. Then she said,

   a. Don't count your chickens before they hatch.

   b. A picture is worth a thousand words.

   c. Take that with a grain of salt.

   d. That was a taste of your
   own medicine.

Penny for your thoughts?

Name: _____   Date: _____

Search for Synonyms

Read each word. Find a synonym for it in the puzzle, circle it, then write it on the blank.

1. glad   _____

2. big   _____

3. giggle   _____

4. gift   _____

5. fast   _____

6. yell   _____

7. easy   _____

8. walk   _____

9. throw   _____

```
E  P  P  S  I  M  P  L  E  U
J  L  Q  U  I  C  K  U  S  K
H  A  P  P  Y  V  V  R  A  Z
B  U  F  R  W  K  P  D  N  C
S  G  C  A  S  C  R  E  A  M
T  H  W  E  P  C  E  L  N  K
R  S  J  T  O  S  S  Y  B  T
O  R  N  F  U  G  E  G  W  A
L  W  U  K  R  Y  N  O  X  V
L  A  R  G  E  D  T  S  M  M
```

Similar Synonyms

Write another synonym for each word.

1. happy   _____

2. large   _____

3. laugh   _____

4. present _____

5. quick   _____

6. scream _____

7. simple _____

8. stroll _____

9. toss   _____

Unscramble the synonym for the underlined word. Then write it on the line.

10. Some people like to be <u>frightened</u> at the movies. *(eascdr)* _____

11. At the library, <u>silence</u> is the rule. *(euiqt)* _____

12. The dog started howling in an <u>eerie</u> way. *(tresnga)* _____

13. Our class <u>transforms</u> its seating plan every month. *(egansch)* _____

14. The kid who stood up to bullies was <u>courageous</u>. *(varbe)* _____

15. You should be extra <u>cautious</u> when crossing a busy street. *(eafrcul)* _____

16. We were <u>anxious</u> about the test on Friday. *(oriwedr)* _____

Antonyms are words that have opposite meanings.
For example, *on* and *off* are antonyms. So are *up* and *down*.

The Antonyms Go Marching

Write the antonyms of the clues in the crossword puzzle.

Across

1. early, on time

3. fearless, brave

6. truth, fact

7. asleep, napping

8. interesting, engaging

Down

2. entrance, way in

3. argue, differ

4. strict, uptight

5. smile, grin

6. dark, pitch-black

More Marching Antonyms

Draw a line to match each word with its antonym.

1. fragile   proud

2. flexible   deep

3. humble   strong

4. obvious   tired

5. create   destroy

6. shallow   messy

7. tidy   stiff

8. alert   hidden

Complete this statement with any pair of antonyms you choose:

I used to be _____, but now I am _____.

Name: _____ Date: _____

Can You Dig It?

Choose words from the box to fill in the blanks.

> culture   artifacts   ancient   crops   resources

How do we learn about people who lived a long time ago? We can learn about what they ate from the _____ that grew there. We can learn about their
(1)

building materials from the _____ that were available to them.
(2)

The most important clues to life in _____ times are the things
(3)

that people made. These objects, or _____, can tell us a lot. The tools
(4)

and art that people left behind help us learn about their _____.
(5)

Name: _____ Date: _____

 Pay attention to important words when you are learning about authors and their work. Those words can help you understand big ideas in literature.

I Spy With My Little Eye

A little road not made of man,
Enabled of the eye,
Accessible to thill of bee,
Or cart of butterfly.

If town it have, beyond itself,
'T is that I cannot say;
I only sigh,—no vehicle
Bears me along that way.

Choose words from the box to fill in the blanks and to learn more about the poem.

> poem   rhyme   poet   stanza   imagines

Emily Dickinson was a famous poet who lived over 100 years ago. That makes the

language she used a little different from ours today. For example, in the first line, "made

of man" means "made by man." Still, you can hear the echo of sounds in the poem

and notice that the words *eye* and *butterfly* _____. In the second
                                                          (1)

_____, notice that the words *say* and *way* do, too.
        (2)

In the first part of the _____, we learn about a tiny little road that
                                    (3)

wasn't made by men. Emily Dickinson _____ that the road is used by
                                                  (4)

bees and butterflies. In the second part, the _____ wonders if the road
                                                          (5)

leads anyplace. She sighs because she is sorry she is too big to explore where it leads!

⭐ Some words can help you when you are learning about the natural world.
Pay attention to words that can help you understand big ideas in science.

Quick Change

Choose words from the box to fill in the blanks.

> landslide   volcano   erosion   erupt   earthquake

The surface of the earth is always changing. It can change slowly over time, as water

and wind wear down the land. That is called _____. But sometimes
(1)

the land changes quickly. For example, the side of a mountain could fall down in a sudden

_____.
(2)

Movement under the surface of the earth causes changes, too. When two giant plates

of land push against each other, one plate can slip. That causes an _____.
(3)

Sometimes hot melted rock from under Earth's surface pushes its way up. That causes a

_____ to _____.
(4)   (5)

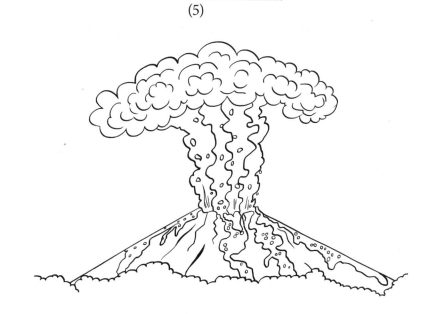

Name: _____ Date: _____

 Some words can help you when you are learning about numbers.
Pay attention to words that can help you understand big ideas in math.

Money Math

Choose words from the box to fill in the blanks.

> hundredths   fraction   decimal   half   tenths

Have you ever thought about how dollars and cents are written? That dot between

dollars and cents is actually a _____ point. Pennies are written
                                        (1)

in the _____ position, and dimes are written in the
          (2)

_____ position.
        (3)

A quarter is 0.25 of a dollar, which is the same as a _____ written
                                                              (4)

like this: ¼. Two quarters equal _____ of a dollar. Paying attention to
                                          (5)

money can help you understand math.

Answer Key

page 7
1. that ate Cleveland
2. who struck out at bat
3. that wore a hat
4. that fell off the shelf
5. who made stone soup
6. that   7. who   8. that

page 8
1. that   2. which   3. which
4. that   5. which
Someone said we should all wear blue hats, which was a silly idea. But none of us have blue hats, which we'd have to buy with our allowance. And you can have school spirit without looking like everyone else, which is the point anyway.

page 9
1. whose   2. who's   3. whose
4. who's   5. whose   6. who's

page 10
1. trying   2. throwing
3. waiting, biting   4. feeling
5. tugging, pulling   6. hoping
7. having

page 11
1. was; have been
2. fell; have fallen
3. threw; have thrown
4. leave; have left
5. play; have played

page 12
Answers will vary. Make sure they conform to column category.

page 13
down; from; around; over; at; under; into; on; of; through
Answer: The zoo

page 14
1. before   2. during   3. after   4. by
5. past   6. since   7. throughout 8. until

```
N  G  T  O (A  F  T  E  R) E
(T  H  R  O  U  G  H  O  U  T)
(P) Y (B  E  F  O  R  E) M  H
(A) T  H  R  G  L  N  C  B  X
(S) V  X  Q (D  U  R  I  N  G)
(T) D  Y (S  I  N  C  E) A  E
 S  Z  D  T (B  Y) S  F  S  O
 G  G  M (U  N  T  I  L) W  Z
```

page 15
1. the basement   2. started a fire
3. made it slippery   4. the windstorm
5. through the wall

page 16
The relay race is about to begin / there are two teams racing / the runners are all fast / everyone is expecting an exciting race / we'll cheer for them all / we hope our school will win
1. The relay race is about to begin, and there are two teams racing.
2. The runners are all fast, so everyone is expecting an exciting race.
3. We'll cheer for them all, but we hope our school will win.

page 17
1. they're   2. to   3. to   4. their
5. their   6. too   7. two   8. to
9. their   10. too   11. there   12. there
13. Your   14. you're 15. Its   16. It's

page 18
Sentences will vary.
Riddle answer: A plain plane

page 19
1. Would/United States Capitol
2. It/Washington/D.C.
3. The/Dr. William Thornton
4. The Capitol/U.S. Congress
5. The/Congress/Senate/House of Representatives
6. The/Congress/Jeannette Rankin/Montana
7. Several/African Americans/Congress/Civil War
8. The/Congress/Elise Stefanik/New York

page 20
1. Ahoy! Talk Like a Pirate Day is on September 19.
2. Dress like someone else on April 20 for Look-Alike Day.
3. May 2 is Brothers and Sisters Day, so be nice!
4. Another date to circle is May 14 for Dance Like a Chicken Day!
5. I can't wait to celebrate National Ice Cream Day on July 21.
6. On August 16, make someone laugh on National Tell a Joke Day.
7. January begins with New Year's Day and ends with Backwards Day!
8. Do your part to support National Stop Bullying Day on October 6.

page 21
1. "Anyone who has never made a mistake has never tried anything new."
2. "Adventure is worthwhile in itself."
3. "You miss 100% of the shots you don't take."
4. "The truth is always the strongest argument."
5. "Freedom is never given; it is won."

page 22
1. Ava yelled ⌃ "Hey, Lamar. Guess what?"
2. Lamar answered⌃ "I can't guess."
3. "I invented a new game⌃" said Ava.
5. "It's called Comma Commando⌃" Ava answered proudly.
7. "Seriously ⌃" said Ava⌃ "do you want to play?"
8. "Well⌃" Lamar said⌃ "it does look like fun."

page 23
| 1. and | 2. so | 3. but |
| 4. and | 5. so | 6. but |

Accept any answer that begins with a conjunction.

page 24
Sample answer: An android is also a robot, but it is designed to look and act like a human. A human would use some conjunctions, so an android would use conjunctions too. Short sentences are for robots.

page 25
1. May	2. can	3. can
4. may	5. can	6. May
7. can	8. may	

page 26
1. Would	2. should	3. should
4. would	5. could	6. could
7. should	8. would	

page 27
1. ascend	2. pleasant	3. realize
4. distant	5. fossil	6. gravel
7. local	8. floral	9. generous
10. protect	11. support	12. tickle

page 28
1. sion	2. sion	3. tion
4. tion	5. sion	6. tion
7. tion	8. sion	9. tion
10. sion	11. sion	12. tion

page 29
1. pair of pears	2. ant aunt	3. bare bear
4. pale pail	5. tick	6. pop
7. row	8. seal	9. palm

page 30
1. present	2. cheese	3. says
4. music	5. news	6. poison
7. artificial	8. glaciers	9. official
10. physician	11. social	12. delicious

page 31
1. Wednesday	2. autumn	3. knight
4. castle	5. half	6. knot
7. thumb	8. listened	9. sign
10. wrong	11. knowing	12. wrong
13. knight	14. sighed	15. walked

page 32
friend, busy, ready, idea, said, beauty, school, pizza

page 33
1. thoughtful	2. frosty
3. witty	4. flavorful
5. sobbing	6. grateful
7. dazzling	8. deafening

page 34
Possible answers:
| 1. Samir, | 2. Wow, | 3. , okay |
| 4. Wait, | 5. , buddy, | 6. , right |

page 35
Joey: Hey, what's up? Got the time? I've gotta be home by five, or else!
Joseph: Hello, how are you? I am not sure what time it is. I am supposed to be home at five, too.
Sample answer (Joseph): I have to go now.
Sample answer (Joey): Later!

page 36

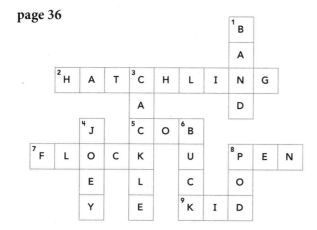

page 37
1. flour   2. deer   3. bored
4. grown   5. flower   6. dear
7. board   8. groan

page 38
1. below   2. half   3. before
4. more or better
5. sub   6. semi
7. fore   8. super

page 39

overfeed	underfeed
overachieve	underachieve
overrated	underrated

1. Yes   2. Yes   3. No
4. No   5. No   6. Yes

page 40
1. speaker   2. teacher   3. hopeless
4. breathless   5. singer   6. fearless
7. headless   8. player

page 41
1. agreeable   2. helpful   3. careful
4. cloudy   5. beatable   6. cheerful
7. dirty   8. electable   9. powerful
10. curly

page 42
1. biography, biology, biodegradable
   Sentences will vary.
2. geology, geometry, geography
   Sentences will vary.
3. photocopy, photograph, photosynthesis
   Sentences will vary.

page 43
4. percent, century
   Sample word: centimeter
5. audience, audition
   Sample word: audio
6. construction, destruct
   Sample word: instruct
7. attract, tractor
   Sample word: attraction

page 44
1. va/por (open)   2. hap/pen (closed)
3. en/gine (closed)   4. me/ter (open)
5. spi/der (open)   6. in/sect (closed)
7. prob/lem (closed)   8. mu/sic (open)
9. ug/ly (closed)   10. hu/man (open)
11. ra/dar (open)   12. ob/ject (closed)

page 45
1. exceptional   2. watermelon
3. animation   4. definitely
5. congratulations   6. encouragement

page 46
1. dis, re, un
2. cover, mark, kind
3. ed, able, ness
Sample words: discovered, remarkable, unkindness

page 47
1. city   2. empty, end
3. object, obvious   4. show
5. left, legend   6. rosy, rotate

page 48
Sample answers:
1. bright   2. twirled   3. soft
4. cried   5. smelly   6. cold

page 49
1. Sample answer: An octopus has eight arms; many arms would help a player block an opponent.
2. Sample answer: A cheetah is fast; being fast would help a runner win a race.

page 50
Sentences will vary. Sample metaphors:
1. The fog was a blanket over the land.
2. The air conditioning made the room into a freezer.
3. The dinosaur of a car still runs.
4. The child was a fish in water.

page 51
1. c   2. b   3. h   4. e
5. a   6. f   7. d   8. g

page 52

1. c 2. a 3. d

page 53

1. happy 2. large 3. laugh
4. present 5. quick 6. scream
7. simple 8. stroll 9. toss

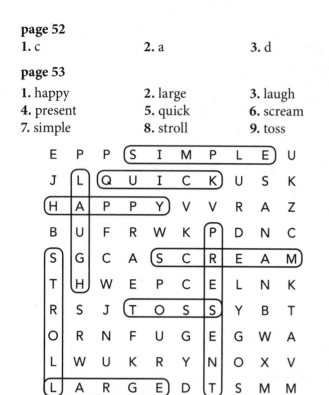

page 54

Sample answers:

1. joyous 2. huge 3. chuckle
4. giveaway 5. speedy 6. shout
7. uncomplicated 8. strut 9. pitch
10. scared 11. quiet 12. strange
13. changes 14. brave 15. careful
16. worried

page 55

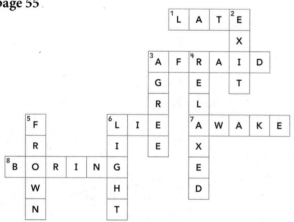

page 56

1. strong 2. stiff 3. proud
4. hidden 5. destroy 6. deep
7. messy 8. tired

Antonym pairs will vary.

page 57

1. crops 2. resources 3. ancient
4. artifacts 5. culture

page 58

1. rhyme 2. stanza 3. poem
4. imagines 5. poet

page 59

1. erosion 2. landslide 3. earthquake
4. volcano 5. erupt

page 60

1. decimal 2. hundredths 3. tenths
4. fraction 5. half